Poultry 1

Cookbook

Please your family with these mouth-watering recipes from grill to stir-fry, for beginners and advanced. This book is thought to let you use free-range and natural-fed animals. Detox your body and satisfy your hunger, with a tasteful surplus and keeping a low budget.

Dorian Gravy

Table of Contents

Welcome, dear hungry buddy!

This is my offer to your cooking style.

This cookbook is the realization of my research on how to eat tasty and healthy food at the meantime.
My purpose is to increase your energies and to let you live a lighter life, without the junk of the globalised kitchen.

In here, you'll find my knowledge on how to create delicious dishes with poultry.

Jump into a worldwide discovery of good food and natural-feed animals, with many recipes for a varied diet.

Nevertheless, you'll learn new techniques, discover tastes of all around the world and improve your skills.
Let yourself be inspired by the worldwide traditions, twisted by a proper chef.

Each of these dishes is thought to:

1 – Let you understand how to work with the meat of poultry

This majestic animal is presented in various dishes of different cultures, to show you how the same ingredient can change from dish to dish.

2 – Balance your weight with different cooking methods

As soon as you learn different ways to cook your meat, you'll discover an entire world of new ideas.
Poultry will never bore you again!

3 – Amaze your friends starting from the smell

Once your friends will come to dinner, they will be in love with your food even before to see your creation.

Poultry Recipes

"When I'm eating fried chicken
I think about nothing else but eating fried chicken.
Everything, in short, makes no sense.
But not the crispy skin on my fried chicken"

Spiced Healthy Chicken

Ingredients

- 1/4 cup light soy sauce
- 1/2 teaspoon whole cloves
- 1 (2-inch) cinnamon stick
- 1 cardamom pod
- 1 whole star anise
- 2 tablespoons sugar
- 1/4 teaspoon dried tangerine peel (dried orange peel can be substituted)
- 1/2 teaspoon whole black peppercorns
- 6 boneless, skinless chicken breasts
- 5 cups water

Procedure

1. Put the star anise, peppercorns, cloves, cinnamon stick, cardamom pod, tangerine peel, and water in a stew pot. Bring the mixture to its boiling point using high heat. Let boil until the poaching liquid is reduced to 4 cups.

2. Mix in the soy sauce and the sugar. Return the liquid to its boiling point.

3. Put in the chicken breasts and reduce to a simmer. Poach the breasts until done, approximately twenty minutes.

Green Thai Curry Chicken

Serves 5 pax

Ingredients

- 1/4 cup vegetable oil
- 2 cups coconut milk
- 3 whole boneless, skinless chicken breasts, cut into bite-sized pieces
- 5 cups Steamed white rice
- 1/4 cup (or to taste) chopped cilantro leaves
- 1/4 cup Green Curry Paste
- 2 tablespoons fish sauce

Procedure

1. Heat 2 tablespoons of vegetable oil in a big sauté pan or wok on moderate heat.
2. Put in the chicken and sauté until mildly browned on all sizes. Take away the chicken and save for later.
3. Put in the remaining vegetable oil to the sauté pan. Mix in the curry paste and cook for two to three minutes.
4. Put in the coconut milk and carry on cooking for five minutes. Put in the reserved chicken and fish sauce.
5. Decrease the heat and simmer until chicken is soft, fifteen to twenty minutes. Mix in the cilantro.
6. Serve with steamed white rice.

Roasted Chicken and Garlic

Serves 2 pax

Ingredients

- Coarse salt and ground pepper
- 2 tablespoons butter, room temperature
- 1 whole chicken (3 to 4 pounds), rinsed and patted dry (giblets removed)
- 40 garlic cloves (3 to 4 heads), unpeeled
- 6 sprigs fresh thyme

Procedure

1. Preheat oven to 475 degrees. Place garlic in a medium bowl; cover with another same-size bowl, creating a dome.

2. Hold bowls together tightly, and shake vigorously until skins are loosened, about 30 seconds. Remove and discard skins; set garlic aside.

3. Place chicken in a large ovenproof skillet or roasting pan. Rub all over with 1 tablespoon butter. Season with salt and pepper.

4. Add thyme, garlic, and remaining tablespoon butter to skillet.

5. Roast, basting occasionally with juices and stirring garlic, until a thermometer inserted in thickest part of a thigh (avoiding bone) registers 165 degrees, 45 to 60 minutes.

6. Transfer to a platter and let rest 10 minutes. Carve chicken and serve with garlic and pan juices.

Tandoori Chicken

Serves 4 pax

Ingredients

- 1 tablespoon grated ginger
- 2 teaspoons <u>Garam Masala</u>
- 2 small garlic cloves, minced
- 1/2 cup plain yogurt
- 1/2 teaspoon saffron threads
- 2 tablespoons ghee, melted
- 4 skinless chicken legs
- 1 teaspoon chili powder
- 2 teaspoons paprika
- 2 teaspoons salt
- 4 skinless chicken breasts

Procedure

1. Using a small, sharp knife, make three to 4 (1/4-inch-deep) slits in each piece of chicken. Set aside in a container big enough to hold all of the pieces.
2. Put the saffron in a small sauté pan on moderate heat and toast for roughly half a minute. Put the saffron on a small plate and let it cool and crumble. Mix the saffron into the yogurt.
3. Grind together the ginger, garlic, garlic, salt, chili pepper, paprika, and garam masala. Mix the spice mixture into the yogurt. Pour the yogurt over the chicken, ensuring that all of the pieces are coated. Cover and marinate overnight flipping the pieces in the marinade every so frequently.
4. Preheat your oven to 450 degrees. Put in the ghee to a roasting pan big enough to hold all of the chicken pieces. Put in the chicken, breast side down. Ladle some of the ghee over the pieces. Roast for about ten minutes. Turn the pieces over, coat again, and continue roasting for five minutes. Turn them again and roast for another five minutes. Turn 1 last time. Coat and cook until done, 5 more minutes.

Tea Smoked Chicken

Serves 7 pax

Ingredients

- 1/2 cup green tea leaves
- 1/2 teaspoon salt
- 8 boneless, skinless chicken breasts
- 1/2 cup brown sugar
- 1/2 cup cooked rice
- 1 teaspoon sesame oil
- 2 teaspoons rice wine

Procedure

1. Swiftly wash the chicken breasts under cold water and pat dry. Drizzle with the salt and rice wine. Set aside in your fridge for half an hour.
2. In the meantime, prepare the wok. Coat the bottom using a sheet of aluminium foil. Put the tea leaves, brown sugar, and rice on the bottom of the wok and toss to blend. Place a wire grill rack on the wok.
3. Heat the wok on moderate to high heat. Place the chicken on the rack and cover with a tight-fitting lid. Remove the heat after smoke starts to emit from the wok, but leave it on the burner for about ten minutes or until the chicken is thoroughly cooked.
4. Brush the chicken with the sesame oil.
5. Serve immediately.

Hot Spicy Noodles

Serves 5 pax

Ingredients

- 2 tablespoons vegetable oil
- 2 whole boneless, skinless chicken breasts, cut into bite-sized pieces
- 2 tablespoons fish sauce
- 20 (or to taste) Thai bird chilies, stemmed and seeded
- 1 (8-ounce) can bamboo shoots, drained
- 2 cups loose-packed basil and/or mint
- 5 (or to taste) cloves garlic
- 1 pound presliced fresh rice noodles
- 2 tablespoons sweet black soy sauce
- 1 tablespoon oyster sauce
- 1 teaspoon white pepper
- 2 tablespoons sugar

Procedure

1. Put the chilies and garlic cloves in a food processor and pulse until meticulously mashed together; set aside.
2. Bring a kettle of water to its boiling point. Put the noodles in a big colander and pour the hot water over them. Cautiously unfold and separate the noodles; set aside.
3. Heat the oil in a wok or big frying pan on moderate to high heat. When it is fairly hot, cautiously put in the reserved chili-garlic mixture and stir-fry for fifteen seconds to release the aromas.
4. Increase the heat to high, put in the chicken, and stir-fry until it starts to lose its color, approximately half a minute. Mix in the fish sauce, soy sauce, oyster sauce, white pepper, and sugar.
5. Put in the noodles and continue to stir-fry for half a minute, tossing them with the other ingredients.
6. Put in the bamboo shoots and cook for one more minute.
7. Remove the heat and put in the basil.

Traditional Soup

Serves 9 pax

Ingredients

- 1 jalapeño, seeded and cut
- 1 tablespoon ground cumin
- 1 (1-inch) cinnamon stick
- 1 (14-ounce) can coconut milk
- 1 tablespoon vegetable oil
- 2 medium onions, peeled
- 2 teaspoons salt
- 5 cups cooked rice
- 2 cardamom pods, bruised
- 3 cups chicken broth
- 2 teaspoons whole peppercorns
- 2 cloves garlic, peeled
- 9 pounds chicken wings
- 2 whole cloves
- Lemon juice to taste

Procedure

1. Put the chicken wings in a big soup pot. Cover the chicken with cold water. Stick the cloves into 1 of the onions and put the onion in the pot with the chicken.
2. Put in the garlic, jalapeño, cinnamon stick, peppercorns, cardamom, cumin, and salt.
3. Bring the mixture to its boiling point, reduce to a simmer, and cook for two to three hours.
4. Allow the stock comes to room temperature. Take away the chicken pieces from the broth and chop the meat from the bones. Set aside the meat.
5. Strain the broth. Thinly slice the rest of the onion.
6. In a big sauté pan, heat the oil on moderate to high heat. Put in the onion slices and sauté until translucent. Put in the curry leaves and the broth. Heat to a simmer and allow to cook for five minutes.

7. Put in enough water to the coconut milk to make 3 cups of liquid. Put in this and the reserved meat to the broth. Heat the soup, but do not allow it to boil. Season to taste with additional salt and a squeeze of lemon juice.

8. To serve, place roughly 1/2 cup of cooked rice on the bottom of each container. Ladle the soup over the rice.

Pea Pods

Serves 6 pax

Ingredients

- 1/4 teaspoon salt
- 2 pounds fresh sugar snap peas
- 1/2 cup chicken broth
- 1/4 teaspoon fresh ground black pepper

Procedure

1. Mix ingredients in large skillet. Bring to a boil.
2. Cover and let simmer 4 minutes. Pea pods are done when crisp and tender.
3. Serve hot.

William Potato

Serves 6 pax

Ingredients

- 3 cups cold mashed Russet potatoes
- 11 egg
- 1 cup breadcrumbs
- 1 strand angel hair spaghetti
- 6 dried bay leaves

Procedure

1. Preheat oven to 375°F.
2. Beat egg lightly. Set aside in shallow dish.
3. Sprinkle breadcrumbs on plate. Set aside.
4. Split mashed potatoes into 6 equal mounds. Take one potato mound and form into a pear shape by hand. Coat potato pear in egg. Roll potato pear in breadcrumbs. Place upright on baking sheet.
5. Repeat process until all mounds of mashed potato are potato pears. Bake 20 minutes in oven. William potatoes are done when golden brown. Remove from oven and transfer to serving platter.
6. Snap spaghetti strand into 6 equal pieces. Stick broken spaghetti strands into tops of potato pears to form stems.
7. Insert bay leaves at top of potato pears to add a leaf to each pear.

Double Curried Coconut Chicken

Serves 2 pax

Ingredients

- 1 teaspoon curry powder
- 2 boneless skinless chicken breast halves (6 ounces each)
- 4 teaspoons butter, melted
- 1/2 cup sweetened shredded coconut
- 1/8 teaspoon salt
- 1/2 cup apricot preserves, warmed

Procedure

1. In a shallow bowl, place butter. Mix curry powder and coconut in another shallow bowl. In butter, dip chicken; coat in coconut mixture.
2. Put into an 11x7-in. greased baking dish and sprinkle with salt.
3. Bake till thermometer reads 30-35 minutes at 350°, uncovered.
4. Serve with preserves.

Oven Duck Breast

Ingredients

- 6 skinless duck breasts
- 4 tablespoons extra-virgin olive oil
- 3/4 teaspoon salt
- 1/2 teaspoon fresh ground white pepper
- 3/4 teaspoon fresh ground coriander
- 1 tablespoon sugar
- 2 cups fresh squeezed orange juice
- 2 tablespoons orange zest
- 1/2 cup Grand Marnier
- 2 cups butter

Procedure

1. Rub duck breasts with olive oil, salt, pepper, and coriander. Wrap breasts in plastic wrap. Refrigerate 2 hours. Place breasts in large skillet on medium heat. Cook 4 minutes each side until browned.

2. Transfer duck breasts to platter. Cover gently with aluminum foil. Let stand 5 minutes.

3. Combine orange juice, sugar, orange zest, and 1/4 cup Grand Marnier in saucepan. Bring to a boil on medium-high heat. Lower heat to medium.

4. Simmer until reduced to 1/4 cup. Remove from heat and whisk in butter, a few pieces at a time. When fully blended, whisk in additional 1/4 cup Grand Marnier.

5. Slice duck diagonally into 1/4" slices.

6. Spoon Grand Marnier sauce onto serving plates. Arrange the duck on top of sauce.

Bucatini with Duck Confit

Serves 6 pax

Ingredients

- 3 ounces onion
- 1 oz grated Parmigiano Reggiano cheese
- 1 tbsp parsley
- 5 ounces red wine
- 3/4 pound fresh bucatini pasta
- 1 tsp salt
- 11 ounces duck meat from confit (recipe follows).
- 2 ounces butter
- 3 ounces ripe tomatoes, chopped
- Thyme to taste
- Marjoram to taste
- 1 bay leaf salt
- Freshly ground black pepper

Procedure

1. Boil a large pot of salted water. Add pasta and cook to al dente while preparing sauce.

2. Melt butter in large skillet. Sauté onions until browned. Add duck meat and mix well. Add wine.

3. Cook on high heat until liquid reduces in half. Add herbs, bay leaf and tomatoes. Season to taste with salt and pepper. Cook 15 minutes on medium-high heat, stirring occasionally.

4. When mixture is saucy, taste and adjust seasoning. While still al dente, drain pasta.

5. Transfer to sauce skillet and toss well. Add parsley. Remove from heat and sprinkle with grated cheese.

6. Garnish with parsley and arrange on serving dishes.

7. Serve with sautéed Mushrooms and diced Zucchini (recipe follows).

Duck Confit

Serves 6 pax

Ingredients

- 1 shallot, peeled and sliced
- 6 sprigs thyme
- 3 tablespoons salt
- 4 garlic cloves, smashed
- Freshly ground black pepper
- 4 duck legs, with thighs
- 4 duck wings, trimmed
- 4 cups duck fat

Procedure

1. Sprinkle 1 tablespoon salt on bottom of large dish. Sprinkle half the shallots, half the thyme and half the garlic in dish.

2. Arrange duck pieces in single layer in dish, skin-side up. Sprinkle remaining salt, garlic, shallots, thyme. Season to taste with pepper. Seal and refrigerate 2 days.

3. Preheat oven to 225°F.

4. Melt duck fat in small saucepan. Remove duck pieces from refrigerator. Brush off salt and seasonings. Place duck pieces in one tight layer in baking dish. Pour melted duck fat over pieces. Duck should be completely covered by fat.

5. Place baking dish in oven. Cook 3 hours. Confit will simmer very slowly. Confit is done when duck is tender and easily pulled from bone. Remove confit from oven. Let duck cool to room temperature in the fat.

6. Refrigerate at least 24 hours. Confit will keep in the refrigerator up to 4 weeks.
7. Before serving, lift duck pieces from fat. Remove and discard skin.
8. Pull duck meat from bone and add to Bucatini (recipe above).

Turkey and Trimmings

Ingredients

- 1/2 cup mixed raisins
- 1/4 cup dried cherries
- 1 young tom turkey (12 pounds)
- 1 pound Hawaiian sweet bread, cubed 1"
- 1/4 cup dried cranberries
- 1/4 cup currants
- 1/4 cup celery, diced
- 2 cups turkey broth
- 1 turkey heart and 1 turkey gizzard
- 1/2 cup honey mead
- Salt and fresh ground black pepper
- 3/4 cup unsalted butter
- 10 tablespoons all-purpose flour
- 2 teaspoons water
- 1 hard-boiled egg, chopped fine

Procedure

1. Cut wing tips from turkey. (Can be used for broth or soup.) Season turkey inside and out with salt and pepper to taste.
2. Put bread cubes, raisins, dried fruit, currants, celery and mead in large bowl. Mix stuffing well.
3. Fill turkey cavity with stuffing. Flex thigh and wing joints and truss turkey with string.
4. Mix 4 tablespoons butter with 4 tablespoons flour. Rub turkey all over with butter-flour mixture. Massage in thoroughly.
5. Sprinkle remaining flour in the bottom of roasting pan. Place roasting rack inside pan. Position turkey breast-up on rack. Let sit 30 minutes.
6. Preheat oven to 450°F. Place roasting pan in oven. Roast 45 minutes.
7. While turkey cooks, melt remaining butter in small saucepan. Add water and stir well. Baste turkey with melted butter mix.

8. Lower heat to 350°F. Roast 1 hour 40 minutes. Baste frequently with melted butter mix. Remove turkey from oven. Let stand 20 minutes. Transfer to carving board.

9. Bring turkey broth to boil in saucepan. Add turkey heart and gizzard. Lower heat to simmer. Cook 10 minutes.

10. Strain. Reserve and set aside broth. Chop giblets fine. Set aside.

11. While turkey stands, skim off semi-transparent liquid from roast pan drippings.

12. Place unwashed roast pan on stove top. Add reserved broth. Scrape pan until browned particles on bottom and sides of pan dissolves.

13. Strain broth into saucepan. Bring to boil. Lower heat to simmer. Cook 10 minutes. Skim surface as needed. Add chopped giblets and egg.

14. Carve turkey and serve with gravy on the side.

Consommé Denise with Tortellini

Serves 8 pax

Ingredients

- 1 onion
- 1/2 pound of carrots
- 15 egg whites
- 1 pound lean ground chicken
- 1/2 pound leeks
- 1/2 pound celery
- 1/2 bunch parsley sprigs
- 2 fresh thyme sprigs
- 1 gallon chicken stock
- 9 ounces cheese tortellini
- 1 cup tomato purée
- 5 black peppercorns
- 2 bay leaves
- Salt and pepper

Procedure

1. Dice onion, carrots, leeks and celery into small cubes. Whip egg whites lightly in a mixing bowl.
2. Combine ground chicken, diced vegetables, tomato purée, herbs, and spices together. Mix in egg whites.
3. Blend chicken stock and meat mix in a stock pot with spigot, Place stock pot on medium heat.
4. Heat to 160 degrees F, stirring occasionally, until a raft forms. Simmer for 90 minutes. Do not allow raft to break up or sink. Open spigot, pour off and discard enough liquid to remove any sediment.
5. Line a china cap strainer with 5 layers of cheesecloth. Strain the liquid slowly through the china cap. Re-line and re-strain as necessary until liquid becomes a clear consommé.
6. Add Tortellini to consommé in a large saucepan. Bring to a boil. Cook 5 minutes uncovered.
7. Tortellini is done when tender, Season to taste with salt and pepper. Garnish with herb sprigs.
8. Serve hot.

Parmantier Cream Soup

Serves 6 pax

Ingredients

- 2 cups cubed potatoes
- 1/4 teaspoon pepper
- Fresh chives for garnish
- 4 tablespoons butter
- 6 tablespoons heavy cream
- 8 cups chicken stock
- 2 cups leeks
- 2 onions
- 1 tablespoon salt

Procedure

1. Clean and dice the white and tender green parts of leeks and onions.

2. Heat butter in a heavy saucepan. Sauté leeks and onions until soft and yellow. Add potatoes, salt, and pepper to chicken stock. Simmer 50 minutes until the potatoes are tender and soft.

3. Transfer to food processor and puree. Reheat and season to taste. Stir in the cream.

4. Ladle soup into serving dishes. Add buttered croutons.

5. Garnish with chives. Serve hot.

Chicken Breast and Peanut Sauce Noodles

Serves 6 pax

Ingredients

- 1/4 cup half-and-half
- 1 cup crispy peanut butter
- 1/4 cup chicken stock
- 1/4 cup lime juice
- 1 pound Chinese egg noodles (mein)
- 1 pound snow peas, trimmed and blanched
- 2 teaspoons brown sugar
- 1 whole boneless, skinless chicken breasts, halved and poached
- 2 cloves garlic, minced
- 1 tablespoon peanut oil
- 1 tablespoon sesame oil
- 2 cups coconut milk
- 2 tablespoons fish sauce

Procedure

1. Mix the peanut butter, coconut milk, fish sauce, lime juice, brown sugar, garlic, salt, and pepper in a small deep cooking pan using low heat. Cook until the desired smoothness is achieved and thick, stirring regularly.

2. Move to a blender and purée. Put in the chicken stock and half-and-half, and blend; set aside.

3. Bring a big pot of water to its boiling point. Put in the noodles and cook until firm to the bite. Drain, wash under cold water, and drain once more. Toss the noodles with the peanut and sesame oils.

4. To serve, place some pasta in the center of each serving plate. Ladle some of the peanut sauce over the pasta.

5. Slice each chicken breast on the diagonal. Move 1 cut breast to the top of each portion of noodles.

6. Ladle some additional peanut sauce over the chicken. Surround the noodles with the snow peas.

Marsala Jus

Serves 6 pax

Ingredients

- 1 sprig fresh thyme
- Salt and fresh cracked black pepper
- 2 tablespoons butter
- 2 cups chicken stock
- 1 clove garlic
- 3/4 cup Marsala wine
- 2 shallots

Procedure

1. Chop garlic and slice shallots. Place in a small saucepan with the thyme. Sauté in just enough butter to cook.
2. Deglaze with Marsala and reduce to a syrup. Add chicken stock and simmer until reduced by one half. Add salt and pepper to taste.
3. Strain and return to saucepan. Whisk in the rest of the butter.
4. Serve.

Asian Chicken and Rice Soup

Serves 7 pax

Ingredients

- 2 tablespoons fish sauce
- 2 whole boneless, skinless chicken breasts, trimmed and slice into fine strips
- 1 tablespoon vegetable oil
- 1 garlic cloves, minced
- 2 teaspoons minced ginger
- 6 cups low-fat, low-salt chicken broth

Procedure

1. In a big soup pot, heat the oil on moderate to high. Put in the chicken strips and sauté for two to three minutes.

2. Put in the garlic and gingerroot and sauté for one more minute. Mix in the fish sauce, broth, and rice. Bring to its boiling point; reduce heat, cover, and simmer for about ten minutes.

3. Put in the green onions and snow peas; simmer to heat through.

4. Adjust seasoning with salt and freshly ground white pepper to taste.

Rice, Chicken and Vegs

Serves 2 pax

Ingredients

For the Noodles:

- 2 tablespoons vegetable oil
- 1 tablespoon sweet black soy sauce
- 8 ounces rice stick noodles

For the Chicken and Vegs:

- 1/4 pound broccoli, chopped
- 1/2 teaspoon Tabasco
- 1/4 cup chicken broth
- 1/4 cup cut green onions
- 1 small onion, finely cut
- 1 small red bell pepper, seeded and slice into strips
- 1 big whole boneless, skinless chicken breast
- 1 cup bean sprouts
- 1 tablespoon cornstarch mixed with

- 1 tablespoon water
- 2 cups cut Japanese eggplant
- 2 tablespoons fish sauce
- 2 tablespoons vegetable oil
- 2 tablespoons Yellow Bean Sauce
- 2 tablespoons brown sugar
- 2 cloves garlic, chopped

Procedure

For the Noodles:

1. Soak the noodles in warm water for fifteen minutes or until soft; drain.
2. Put a wok on moderate to high heat and put in the vegetable oil. Once the oil is hot, put in the noodles and stir-fry vigorously until they are thoroughly heated, approximately 45 seconds to one minute.
3. Put in the soy sauce and continue to stir-fry for 1 more minute. Put the noodles on a serving platter, covered in foil, in a warm oven until ready to serve.

For the Chicken and Vegs:

1. Put a wok on moderate to high heat and put in the vegetable oil. Once the oil is hot, put in the garlic and stir-fry for a short period of time to release its aroma.

2. Put in the chicken and cook until it begins to become opaque. Put in the broccoli and stir-fry for half a minute. Put in the onion and eggplant and stir-fry for a couple of minutes. Put in the Tabasco, fish sauce, yellow bean sauce, and sugar. Stir-fry for a minute.

3. Put in the broth, cornstarch mixture, bean sprouts, green onions, and red bell pepper; cook until vegetables are soft-crisp.

4. To serve, ladle the chicken and vegetable mixture over the reserved noodles.

Royal Vol-au-Vent

Serves 6 pax

- 1 tablespoon water
- 3 large chicken breasts
- 1/2 pound puff pastry
- 1 egg, beaten
- 2 cups veal
- 3 bay leaves
- 2 cloves
- 1 teaspoon sea salt
- 1 teaspoon nutmeg
- 2 cups fresh mushrooms
- 1 teaspoon peppercorns
- 2 tablespoons butter
- 1/2 cup all-purpose flour
- 1/2 cup chicken stock
- 1/2 cup white wine

Procedure

1. Chill 1/2 pounds of puff pastry. Line baking sheet with parchment paper. Lightly flour a clean work surface. Roll dough into a rectangle 3/8" thick. Transfer to baking sheet. Refrigerate 10 minutes.

2. Use a 3" cutter to cut 12 circles of dough. Use a 11/2" cutter to cut centers from six rounds to form rings for the sides of the vols-au-vent.

3. Set center cuts aside for caps. Mix beaten egg and water well to create egg wash. Lightly prick solid rounds with fork. Do not perforate. Brush lightly with egg wash. Place dough rings on top of bottom rounds and press lightly, forming sides.

4. When adhered, brush top rings lightly with egg wash. Prick and egg wash the caps. Refrigerate assembled vols-au-vent on lined baking sheet.

5. Preheat oven to 400°F. Remove from refrigerator and cover with silicon baking mat. Bake vols-au-vent 15 minutes until risen and starting to brown.

6. Lower oven to 350°F. Remove silicon mat. Gently press down any risen centers. Bake 15 minutes uncovered.

7. Vol-au-vent shells are done when layers are golden brown. Caps will bake faster than the shells. Remove when done. Remove shells to cooling rack.

8. Put chicken, veal, bay leaves, cloves and peppercorns in large pot of cold water. Bring to slow boil, Lower heat to medium-low. Cook 2 hours. Combine butter and flour. Sauté into a roux for the sauce.

9. Thicken sauce with chicken stock to desired consistency. Season to taste with salt, pepper and nutmeg. Cut meats into small cubes. Sauté mushrooms in butter. Add white wine.

10. Combine everything into the sauce. Mix well. Warm the vol-au-vent shells. Fill warmed vol-au-vent shells and serve hot.

Sautéed Mushrooms and diced Zucchini

Serves 6 pax

Ingredients

- 2 ounces butter
- 3 small zucchini
- 1 cup Extra virgin olive oil
- 2 pounds mushrooms
- 1 cup dry red wine
- 3 garlic cloves

Procedure

1. Clean and halve mushrooms. Dice zucchini into small cubes. Place mushrooms and zucchini in large skillet. Drizzle with olive oil.
2. Add butter. Stir well. Add garlic.
3. Cover skillet and sauté. When mushrooms are cooking well, pour in red wine. Cook until wine evaporates. Mushrooms are done when garlic caramelizes.

Pan-Fried Chicken and Mushrooms

Serves 5 pax

Ingredients

- 2 pounds chicken breasts and legs
- 6 ounces dried Chinese mushrooms
- 2 tablespoons vegetable oil
- 1/2 teaspoon grated ginger
- 1 cup water
- 2 teaspoons sugar
- 4 cloves garlic, crushed

Procedure

1. Put the dried mushrooms in a container, cover with boiling water, and allow to soak for half an hour Drain the mushrooms and wash under cold water; drain again and squeeze dry. Remove any tough stems. Chop the mushrooms into bitesized pieces; set aside.
2. Put the vegetable oil in a wok or big frying pan on moderate to high heat. Put in the garlic and the ginger and stir-fry for a short period of time.
3. Put in the chicken and fry until the skin turns golden. Mix in the water and the sugar. Put in the mushrooms.
4. Lower the heat to low, cover, and cook until the chicken is soft, approximately 30 minutes.

Roasted Capon

Serves 2 pax

Ingredients

- 2 lemons
- 2 tablespoons lemon juice
- 1/4 cup fresh chopped thyme
- 8 pounds capon
- 2 cups water
- Salt and fresh ground black pepper
- 1/4 pound unsalted butter, softened
- 1 onion
- 4 garlic cloves, smashed
- Fresh whole thyme and savory sprigs

Procedure

1. Preheat oven to 450 degrees. Remove neck and giblets from the capon, trim excess fat. Rinse with cold water, inside and out. Pat dry.
2. Season generously with salt and pepper, including the cavity. In a small bowl, blend butter, lemon juice and chopped herbs. Rub the herbed butter all over the capon. Cut lemons and onion in half.
3. Place the lemon halves, onion halves, garlic and whole herbs inside the cavity. Tie legs together with kitchen twine to hold its shape. Place the capon, breast side down, on a rack in a roasting pan.
4. Pour water into the pan. Roast for 20 minutes, then remove from oven. Turn capon breast side up and baste all over with pan drippings. Lower heat to 375 degrees. Return the pan to the oven and roast 2 hours. When done, a meat thermometer in the thick of the thigh reads 165-170 degrees.
5. Remove the bird to a serving platter. Let stand for 15 minutes before carving. Reserve drippings for gravy

Chipolata Stuffing

Serves 6 pax

Ingredients

- 1/2 cup chopped green sweet pepper
- 1/2 cup chopped celery
- 1/2 cup butter
- 1 teaspoon poultry seasoning
- 1/8 teaspoon black pepper
- 2 cups chicken broth
- 12 ounces bulk chipolata sausage meat (recipe follows)
- 3/4 cup finely chopped onion
- 5 cups dry white bread cubes
- 4 cups crumbled corn bread

Procedure

1. In a large skillet, brown sausage over medium heat. Drain, remove from skillet and set aside. In same skillet, sauté onion, sweet pepper, and celery in hot butter over medium heat until tender. Set aside.

2. Combine bread cubes and corn bread in a large bowl. Add cooked sausage, onion mixture, poultry seasoning and black pepper. Drizzle with enough broth to moisten. Toss lightly until combined.

3. Place mixture into a 2-quart casserole dish. Cover and bake in a 325°F oven for 45 minutes or until heated throughout.

Turkey in a Bell Peppers

Serves 5 pax

Ingredients

- 1.25 lbs 99% lean ground turkey
- 5 Bell peppers
- 1.5 cups Breadcrumbs
- 2 tsp Ground cumin
- 1 tsp Italian seasoning
- 1.75 cups Lactose-free cheddar cheese
- 2 tsp Olive oil
- 1 Onion
- 1/4 tsp Paprika
- Pepper and salt
- 2 Tomatoes

Procedure

1. This recipe bakes best at 325° F, so prepare accordingly. Cut your peppers in half longways. Remove all seeds and then set your peppers on a greased sheet pan.
2. Place a greased skillet on medium-high heat and cook the ground turkey with the seasonings, garlic, and onion. Crumble any large chunks.
3. Lower the temperature and toss in the tomato, breadcrumbs, and cheese.
4. Scoop the turkey mixture into the bell peppers and add a dash of paprika on top. Bake for 20 minutes.
5. Serve.

Chicken Salad

Serves 4 pax

Ingredients

For the dressing:

- 1 tablespoon soy sauce
- 2 Tablespoons rice wine vinegar
- 1/4 cup vegetable oil
- 1/2 teaspoon salt
- 2 teaspoons grated gingerroot
- A pinch of sugar

For the salad:

- 1 tablespoon toasted sesame seeds
- 2 cups chopped cooked chicken
- 1 cup bean sprouts
- 1 medium head of Chinese cabbage, shredded
- 1 green onions, trimmed and cut
- 3 ounces snow peas, trimmed

Procedure

1. Put the salad dressing ingredients in a small container and whisk vigorously to blend.
2. In a moderate-sized-sized container, mix the chicken, snow peas, green onions, and bean sprouts. Put in the dressing and toss to coat.
3. To serve, position the cabbage on a serving platter. Mound the chicken salad over the cabbage. Decorate using the sesame seeds.

Buttery Lemon Turkey

Serves 12 pax

Ingredients

- 3/4 cup butter, melted
- 1 teaspoon sugar
- 1 teaspoon salt
- 1/2 cup lemon juice
- 2 teaspoons paprika
- 1/2 teaspoon pepper
- 1/4 teaspoon ground mustard
- 1/8 teaspoon hot pepper sauce
- 1 turkey (10 to 12 pounds)

Procedure

1. Set the oven for preheating to 325°. Whisk together the first eight ingredients in a small bowl until well combined; save a quarter cup of mixture for basting the turkey after roasting.

2. Position the turkey on a rack placed in a shallow roasting pan with its breast side facing up. Fold wings underneath the turkey, tying the drumsticks together. Roast without placing any cover for roughly 2 hours while brushing from time to time using the rest of the butter mixture.

3. Continue to roast for about 30-60 minutes more or until a thermometer poked in thickest part of thigh reaches 170°-175°. Baste from time to time using the pan drippings.

4. Take the turkey out from the oven. Heat the reserved butter mixture to melt the butter and brush it on top of the turkey. Tent the turkey using a foil.

5. Let it rest for roughly 20 minutes before cutting.

6. Serve.

Coconut Pumpkin and Chicken Soup

Serves 4 pax

Ingredients

- 4 lb Pumpkin, cubed
- 1 Red bell pepper
- 14 oz Lite coconut milk
- Cilantro
- 1 Lime
- 1 Onion
- 2 Garlic cloves
- An inch long nub Ginger
- 2 cups Chicken broth
- 1 lb Chicken breast
- 1 Tbsp Coconut oil
- Zucchini
- Salt and pepper

Procedure

1. Add a healthy amount of pepper and salt to the chicken breast slices.

2. Heat your coconut oil in a larger pan over a high flame. Stir-fry your meat, browning on both sides and making sure it is cooked through.

3. Stir in the sliced onion, garlic, and ginger. Cook for an additional two minutes. Once done, introduce the cubed pumpkin and zucchini.

4. Add the remaining ingredients and, stirring regularly, get the mixture boiling. Once boiling, reduce heat to simmer. Remove from heat when the pumpkin turns soft.

5. Garnish with cilantro.

Roasted Turkey and Orange

Serves 12 pax

Ingredients

- 1/2 cup packed brown sugar
- 1/4 cup grated orange zest
- 1 cup unsweetened apple juice
- 1/2 cup orange juice
- 1 turkey (12 to 14 pounds)
- 1/2 cup butter, softened
- 1/2 teaspoon ground ginger
- 1 large navel orange, quartered
- 1 large apple, quartered
- 1 small onion, quartered

Procedure

1. Set the oven to 325° and start preheating. On a rack in a shallow roasting pan, put turkey with breast side up. Mix ginger, orange zest, brown sugar and butter together in a small bowl.

2. Use fingers to loosen skin carefully from turkey breast; rub under skin with some of the butter mixture. Use toothpicks to secure skin to underside of breast.

3. Rub the inside of turkey cavity with remaining butter and fill with onion, apple and orange. Tuck wings under turkey; tie together drumsticks. Pour juices carefully over turkey.

4. Bake without a cover until the thermometer inserted in the thickest part of thigh reads 170°-175°, about 3 to 3-3/4 hours, basting with pan drippings occasionally. Use foil to loosely cover to prevent turkey from overbrowning.

5. Cover and allow to sit 20 minutes before carving. Remove onion and fruit from cavity.

6. Skim fat and thicken pan juices as preferred.

7. Serve.

Ultimate Chicken Salad

Serves 3 cups

Ingredients

- 1/2 teaspoon sesame oil
- 1 (1/4-inch) piece ginger, peeled and minced
- 1/2 cup soy sauce
- 1/2 cup celery
- 1 clove garlic, minced
- 1 cup cooked chicken meat
- 1 teaspoon vegetable oil
- 2 tablespoons rice vinegar
- 1 scallion, thinly cut
- 1 tablespoon sugar
- 2 cups shredded bok choy

Procedure

1. In a moderate-sized-sized container, toss together the chicken, bok choy, celery, and scallion.
2. In a small container, meticulously whisk together the rest of the ingredients.
3. Pour over the salad and toss thoroughly to blend.

Lemon and Dill Chicken

Serves 6 pax

Ingredients

- 1 teaspoon dill
- 1/2 cup shredded cheddar cheese
- 3 tablespoons butter, melted, divided
- 6 eggs
- 1 cup milk
- 2 medium carrots, chopped
- 1 cup fresh broccoli florets
- 1 medium onion, chopped
- 1 cup all-purpose flour
- 1/2 teaspoon salt
- 1 tablespoon butter
- 2 cups cubed cooked chicken
- 1 can (10 ounces) condensed cream of chicken soup
- 1 medium sweet red pepper, diced
- 1 tablespoon lemon juice

Procedure

1. Brush 1 tbsp. butter on bottom of deep-dish pie plate; put aside. Mix salt and flour in a small bowl. Beat in leftover butter, milk and eggs till smooth; put into prepped pie plate.
2. Bake for 20 minutes at 400°. Lower heat to 350°; bake till middle is set and golden brown for 5-10 minutes.
3. Meanwhile, microwave butter, onion, broccoli and carrots in a microwave-safe bowl for 5-10 minutes on high, covered, till veggies are crisp tender; put aside.
4. Microwave dill, lemon juice, red pepper, soup and chicken in separate microwave-safe bowl for 3-4 minutes on high till red pepper is tender, mixing once, covered; mix in 1/2 veggie mixture and cheese.
5. Put chicken mixture into middle of popover; surround using leftover veggie mixture.
6. Cut to wedges; immediately serve.

Rosemary Sour Chicken

Serves 6 pax

Ingredients

- 3 garlic cloves, minced
- 1 teaspoon grated grapefruit zest
- 1/2 teaspoon salt, divided
- 1/2 teaspoon pepper, divided
- 1 roasting chicken (6 to 7 pounds)
- 1 medium onion, cut into wedges
- 2 tablespoons grated onion
- 1 tablespoon minced fresh rosemary
- 2 teaspoons minced fresh marjoram
- 1 small pink grapefruit, cut into wedges
- 3 fresh rosemary sprigs
- 3 fresh marjoram sprigs
- 2 tablespoons olive oil

Procedure

1. Mix the first 5 ingredients in a small bowl. Put in 1/4 teaspoon pepper and 1/4 teaspoon salt; put aside.

2. Transfer chicken to a rack in a shallow roasting pan. Sprinkle remaining pepper and salt inside cavity; fill it with grapefruit wedges and onion.

3. Loosen the skin of the chicken breast from both sides carefully using fingers.

4. Arrange marjoram sprigs and rosemary under the skin. Brush oil over the chicken; rub it with prepared herb mixture.

5. Bake at 325° without a cover for 2-1/2 to 3 hours or until a thermometer reads 180°.

6. Allow to rest for 10-15 minutes. Remove the contents of cavity and herb sprigs before slicing.

Grilled Chicken Salad and Forest Dressing

Serves 4 pax

Ingredients

For the Salad:

- Freshly ground black pepper
- 4 skinned chicken breast fillets
- 1 cup olive oil
- salad greens for 4 servings

The dressing:

- 1 tbsp runny honey
- 3 tbsp olive oil
- 2 tbsp raspberry vinegar
- 2 tbsp walnut oil
- Salt and freshly ground black pepper

Procedure

1. Prepare the chicken by lightly brushing each breast with olive oil and seasoning well with pepper.

2. Grill these on the barbie or in a griddle pan until just cooked through and put aside in a warm place to rest for 5 minutes or so.

3. In the meantime, whisk together your dressing ingredients and season – feel free to adjust the quantities of oils, vinegar and seasoning to suit your taste.

4. Plate up your salad greens into stacks. Slice the chicken across the grain into strips ($1/2$in) wide and place on top of the greens.

5. Dress the salad and serve.

Pecaned Chicken Breast

Serves 4 pax

Ingredients

- 0.25 tsp Salt
- 1 Tbsp Spicy brown mustard
- 3 Tbsp Unsweetened applesauce
- 4x 6 oz Boneless, skinless chicken breasts
- 0.5 cups Pecan pieces

Procedure

1. Pulse the pecans until they resemble coarse crumbs. Place in a shallow dish.
2. Place the chicken on a rimmed baking tray lined with parchment baking paper. Mix the applesauce and spicy mustard in a small bowl, then spoon it onto each breast, using the back of the spoon to spread it evenly.
3. One piece at a time, press the sauce-coated side of the chicken into the pecans, then place coated side up on the baking sheet.
4. Press any remaining pecans firmly into the chicken. Sprinkle with salt.
5. Bake at 425° Fahrenheit about 20 minutes until the internal temperature of the chicken reaches 165° Fahrenheit.
6. Serve.

Instant Pot Chili Chicken

Serves 8 pax

Ingredients

- 1 Tbsp Vegetable oil
- 1 Yellow onion
- 4 Garlic cloves
- 1 tsp Cumin
- 1 tsp Oregano
- 2.5 lbs Chicken breast, boneless/skinless
- 16 oz Salsa verde

For the Topping

- 1/2 cup Queso fresco
- 2 Avocado
- 8 Radishes
- 8 sprigs Cilantro

Procedure

1. Turn your Instant Pot onto Saute on medium. Then, add in your vegetable oil, along with the onions. Stir frequently for 3 minutes until soft. Toss in the garlic, then stir another minute. Add in cumin and oregano, then stir another minute.

2. Toss in ½ of the salsa verde. Then, top with chicken breasts before topping with the rest of the salsa on top of the chicken.

3. Put your lid onto the Instant Pot and set the valve to sealing. Choose "manual" and set the timer for 10 minutes. When the timer is up, allow the pressure to release naturally (between 8 and 10 minutes).

4. When the pressure has been released, open the lid, remove the chicken to a bowl, and shred with a fork. Put the chicken back in the pot and stir to incorporate into other ingredients.

5. Serve topped with 1 Tbsp. queso fresco, ¼ avocado (diced), a chopped radish, and a sprig of cilantro.

Buttered Lime Chicken

Serves 6 pax

Ingredients

- 1/2 cup dry vermouth
- 1/4 teaspoon salt
- 1/4 teaspoon pepper
- 4 medium limes
- 1/4 cup sliced almonds, toasted
- 6 chicken breasts (5 ounces each)
- 1/4 cup butter, softened
- 1/4 cup heavy whipping cream

Procedure

1. Preheat an oven to 350°. From 1 lime, grate peel finely. From all limes, squeeze juice to get 1/2 cup; for lime butter, keep 2 tbsp. juice. Mix reserved lime juice, salt and vermouth in a small bowl.
2. Put chicken breasts into an ungreased 13x9-in. baking dish; spread vermouth mixture over the chicken. Bake without cover for 20-25 minutes till fish starts to be easily flaked with a fork.
3. For lime butter, beat cream and butter till fluffy in a small bowl.
4. Add reserved juice slowly; mix in pepper and lime peel.
5. Serve with meat and sprinkle with almonds.

Breakfast Turkey Sausages

Serves 7 pax

Ingredients

- 0.25 tsp Salt
- 1 Tbsp Maple syrup
- A pinch of Black pepper
- 0.5 tsp Poultry seasoning
- 1 lb Lean ground turkey
- 0.5 Tbsp Parsley
- 25 tsp Onion powder
- 1 tsp Fennel seeds

Procedure

1. Toss each of the fixings into a large mixing container. Work the mixture to create 14 two-inch patties.

2. Fry the patties in a large skillet using the med-low temperature setting until it's no longer pink in the center (3-5 min. each side). It will probably be necessary to cook them in batches.

3. Serve hot.

Turkey Spaghetti and Noodles

Serves 5 pax

Ingredients

- 1 tsp Olive oil
- 1.25 lbs Turkey breast
- 1 cup Bell pepper
- 1 Tbsp Garlic
- 2 tsp Italian seasoning
- 0.5 tsp Black pepper
- 0.25 tsp Salt
- 0.25 tsp Red pepper flakes
- 3 cups Marinara sauce
- 2 cups Baby spinach
- 4 Zucchini

Procedure

1. Prepare a large, heavy-bottomed cast-iron pan with olive oil on a moderate heat.
2. Throw in your ground turkey, green pepper, Italian seasoning, garlic, pepper, salt, and red pepper flakes.
3. Allow cooking until turkey is lightly browned, roughly 5 minutes.
4. Mix in your marinara and baby spinach. Cook until the marinara is warm.
5. Mix in the zucchini noodles with tongs. Then, stir and cook until the zucchini is tender, between 2 and 3 minutes.
6. Serve.

Turkey, Bacon and Avocado Toasts

Serves 2 pax

Ingredients

- 1 Plum tomato, sliced thin
- A pinch of Black pepper
- A pinch of Salt
- 2 slices Whole grain bread, toasted
- 1 Avocado
- 2 slices Lean turkey bacon

Procedure

1. Lightly spritz a skillet with a cooking oil spray and add it to a burner using the medium temperature setting.
2. Cook the bacon for 4 minutes per side, until crispy, then place on paper towels to drain.
3. Spread half of the avocado on each slice of bread with a fork, mashing it as flat as possible. Lightly salt and pepper.
4. Place 1 slice of bacon and half of the tomato on each piece of bread.
5. For a no-cook breakfast, cook the bacon in advance and keep it in the fridge.

Herb Roasted Turkey

Serves 12 pax

Ingredients

- 1 (10 pounds) turkey
- 1 teaspoon salt
- 1 teaspoon freshly ground pepper
- 2 cups aromatics, onion, apple, lemon and/or orange, cut into 2-inch pieces
- 1/4 cup fresh herbs, plus 20 whole sprigs, such as thyme, rosemary, sage, oregano and/or marjoram, divided
- 2 tablespoons canola, oil
- 3 cups water, plus more as needed

Procedure

1. In the bottom third of oven, position a rack; preheat an oven to 475 °F.

2. Take neck and giblets off turkey cavities and save for creating gravy. On rack in big roasting pan, put the turkey, breast-side facing up; pat it dry using paper towels.

3. In a small bowl, mix pepper, salt, oil and minced herbs. Rub the entire turkey with herb mixture, beneath skin and on breast meat. In the cavity, put 10 of herb sprigs and aromatics.

4. Fold wing tips beneath turkey. Using kitchen string, bind legs together. In the pan, put the leftover 10 herb sprigs and 3 cups of water.

5. Let the turkey roast for 45 minutes, or till skin turn golden brown.

6. Take turkey out of the oven. Insert remote digital thermometer into the deepest portion of thigh, near joint if using it.

7. With double layers of foil, cover the breast, trimming as needed to fit the breast. Lower the oven heat to 350 °and keep roasting for an additional of 1 1/4 to 1 3/4 hours.

8. Tilt the turkey to allow the juices to flow out of cavity into pan and put in a cup water in case the pan dries. Turkey is done once thermometer or an instant-read thermometer inserted into the thickest portion of thigh but not reaching the bone reads 165°F.

9. On serving platter, put the turkey and cover in foil. In case you're preparing Herbed Pan Gravy, begin here.

10. Allow the turkey to sit for 20 minutes. Take off string and carve.

Classic Stuffed Turkey

Serves 12 pax

Ingredients

- 1 can (14-1/2 ounces) chicken broth
- 1/3 cup minced fresh parsley
- 2 teaspoons rubbed sage
- 1 teaspoon salt
- 1 teaspoon poultry seasoning
- 2 large onions, chopped
- 2 celery ribs, chopped
- 1/2 pound fresh mushrooms, sliced
- 1/2 cup butter
- 1/2 teaspoon pepper
- 12 cups unseasoned stuffing cubes
- Warm water
- 1 turkey (14 to 16 pounds)
- Melted butter

Procedure

1. Sauté mushrooms, celery and onions in butter till tender in a big skillet. Add seasonings and broth; stir well. Put bread cubes into a big bowl.
2. Add the mushroom mixture; toss till coated. Mix in enough warm water to get desired moistness.
3. Loosely stuff turkey then bake. Put any leftover stuffing into a greased baking dish and cover; refrigerate till baking time.
4. Skewer turkey openings; use kitchen string to tie drumsticks together. Put onto a rack in a roasting pan, breast side up; brush with melted butter.
5. Bake without cover for 3 3/4-4 1/2 hours at 325° till a thermometer reads 165° for the stuffing and 180° for the turkey, occasionally basting using pan drippings (if turkey browns very quickly, loosely cover with foil).
6. Bake extra stuffing for 30-40 minutes, covered. Uncover; bake till lightly browned for 10 minutes.

7. Use foil to cover turkey; stand for 20 minutes prior to carving and removing stuffing.
8. Thicken pan drippings for the gravy, if desired.
9. Serve.

Chicken Salad Remastered

Serves 4 pax

Ingredients

- 1 cup cut scallions
- 1 tablespoon dry sherry
- 1 tablespoon soy sauce
- 1/4 cup chopped cilantro, plus extra for decoration
- 1/4 pound rice sticks
- 1 tablespoon vegetable oil
- 2 tablespoons sesame seeds, toasted
- 2 tablespoons lime juice
- 4 Bibb or romaine lettuce leaves
- 1 teaspoon sesame oil
- 1 whole boneless, skinless chicken breasts
- 2 tablespoons hoisin sauce, divided
- 3 tablespoons peanuts, chopped
- Peanut oil for frying

Procedure

1. Mix 1 tablespoon of the hoisin sauce, the soy sauce, and the sherry in a moderate sized container. Put in the chicken breasts and marinate for twenty minutes to half an hour.
2. Heat the vegetable oil in a big frying pan on moderate to high heat. Put in the chicken breasts, saving for later the marinade. Brown the breasts on both sides. Put in the reserved marinade to the frying pan, cover, and cook on moderate to low heat until soft, approximately twenty minutes.
3. Allow the chicken to cool completely, then shred it into bite-sized pieces; set aside.
4. In a moderate-sized-sized container, mix the shredded chicken with the rest of the hoisin sauce, the lime juice, sesame oil, sesame seeds, peanuts, scallions, and cilantro. Put in the shredded chicken and stir to coat.
5. Put in roughly an inch of peanut oil to a big frying pan and heat on high until the oil is hot, but not smoking.

6. Put in the rice sticks cautiously and fry for roughly 6 to 8 seconds or until puffed and golden; turn the rice sticks using tongs and fry for another 6 to 8 seconds.
7. Take away the rice sticks to a stack of paper towels to drain.
8. Toss about of the rice sticks with the chicken mixture.
9. To serve, place a mound of salad on a lettuce leaf on the center of each plate.
10. Top with the rest of the rice sticks and decorate with additional cilantro.

Thank you, *dear meat lover.*

I am glad you accepted my teachings.

These meals have been personally codified in my worldwide trips.

I wanted to share them with you, to let people know more about meat and how to treat it properly.

Now you had come to know about Poultry in all of its shapes, let me give you one more tip.

This manual takes part of an unmissable cookbooks collection.

These meat-based recipes, mixed to all the tastes I met around the world, will give you a complete idea of the possibilities this world offers to us.

You have now the opportunity to add hundreds new elements to your cooking skills knowledge.

Check out the other books!

Dorian Gravy